The Stage Is Set!

Written by Nicolas Brasch

Contents

Harcourt Achieve

Rigby • Saxon • Steck-Vaughn

www.HarcourtAchieve.com
1.800.531.5015

Chapter Snapshots

3 Budget PAGE 18

Money is really important when it comes to designing and building a set. Learn how to use your budget wisely!

4 Time PAGE 24

Time influences the set you end up with. If you only have a short time before you have to perform, you are going to have to take some shortcuts. Here are a few good hints.

5 Imagination PAGE 28

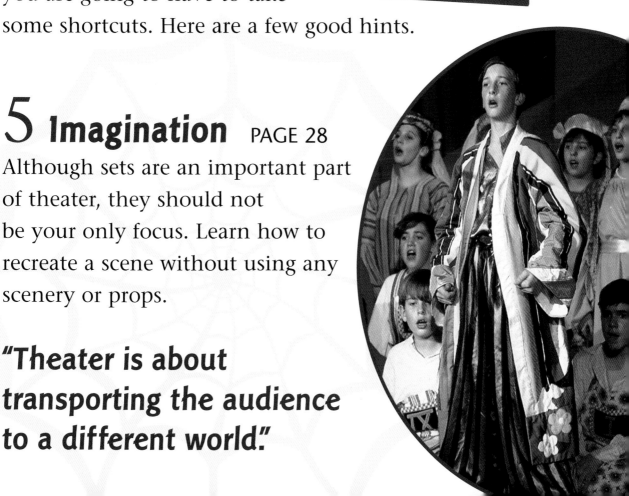

Although sets are an important part of theater, they should not be your only focus. Learn how to recreate a scene without using any scenery or props.

"Theater is about transporting the audience to a different world."

1 Space

In the theater of ancient Greece, a chorus of performers would describe the action to the audience. In this book, a chorus of fourth-grade students explains how they decided on the sets for their theater production. They also give hints for you to follow.

Room to Move

Over the past six weeks, we have been designing and building sets for our play. It took a lot of thought and discussion—and a few arguments! At first, we had no idea of some of the things we had to think about, like making sure that every member of the audience can see all of the performers.

We had to make sure that the stagehands could move the sets between scenes and that the actors could move on and off the stage easily.

"the chorus"

Look at Our Sets!

We have just finished building our sets. We were going to wait until the end of the book before showing them to you, but we're too excited. We love them! We think they fit our space perfectly. As you read this book, you'll discover why we made the sets look this way.

a street sign

a skyscraper

Health and Safety

The job of being a stagehand has changed in recent years. There is now a lot of attention paid to their health and safety. Stagehands use trolleys and other equipment to move heavy loads. This is to protect their backs from injury.

Inside or Outside?

The first decision we had to make was whether to perform the play inside or outside. Some people thought that performing outside would be great because we could take advantage of natural features, such as trees and rocks. However, we eventually decided to perform in the school hall because it might rain on the night we perform.

Amphitheaters

The ancient Greeks and Romans performed plays outside in amphitheaters. An amphitheater is an oval or circular-shaped piece of land surrounded by rising land. This is a very famous ancient amphitheater in Greece, called the Epidaurus.

Large or Small?

Next, we had a long discussion about whether to have a small stage or a large one. Some of us acted out parts of the play on different-sized stages, while others watched and noted the differences. We found that audience members can concentrate better if they have a smaller space to look at.

Proscenium Arch Stage

Our director then told us about the different-shaped stages we could have. We spent a day moving blocks and chairs around the hall, filling up the space in different ways. First, we created a proscenium [pro-se-ne-um] arch stage. This is where the actors perform on a raised, rectangular space in front of the audience.

A proscenium arch stage at Queen's Theatre, Château de Versailles, France.

A proscenium arch stage layout

Thrust Stage

Then we created a "theater-in-the-round." This is where the audience members sit in a circle around the stage. Finally, we created a thrust stage, where the stage juts into the audience. We decided on the thrust stage because the audience is close, but we could still have a backstage area.

This is a theater-in-the-round stage.

This is a thrust stage.

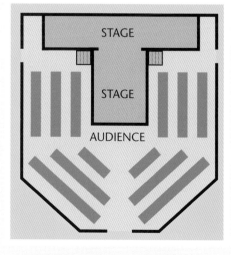

A thrust stage layout

9

2 Examining the Play

Finding Clues in the Play

When you are deciding what type of set to design and build, one of the first things you should do is a close read of the play you are going to be performing. As you read through it, you will find clues that will help you create the most suitable set.

Using Lights

One way of creating a particular atmosphere in a play is to shine a colored light onto the stage. An orange light suggests warmth, while a blue light suggests coolness.

Among the things to look for when you study your play are:
- the type of play it is,
- where the play is set,
- what the characters say, and
- instructions from the playwright.

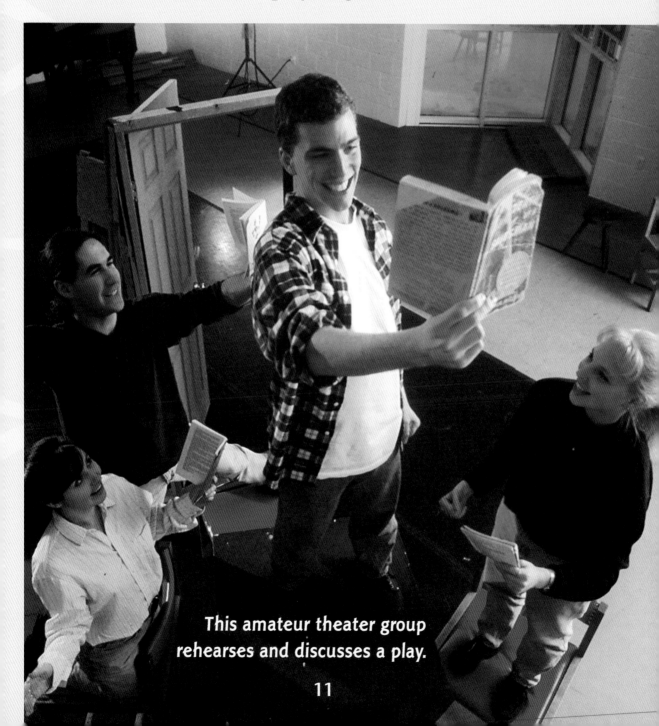

This amateur theater group rehearses and discusses a play.

Type of Play

If you are performing an opera, you will probably have to build an elaborate set. Large sets and fancy costumes are often an important part of opera. If you are performing a naturalistic play, you should make the set look as real as possible. The audience should think they are watching a real event, not a play.

Opera

Opera is an art form that combines music and theater. An orchestra plays the music while performers sing and act on stage. The very first opera was called *Dafne* and it was performed in Italy in 1597.

The Setting

If your play is set in a forest, then your set could be colored green and brown. You could collect sticks and leaves from the park and spread them around the stage. If your play is set in Antarctica, you will have to find a way to represent water and ice.

The Dialogue

Dialogue is the words that the characters speak. These words can give clues to the type of set you might need. For example, a character might be a princess from a fairy tale. Most scenes that take place with that character would need to have the appropriate setting, such as a palace.

Instructions from the Playwright

A play script does not just contain lines of dialogue. Playwrights also indicate where the action is to take place. Sometimes a scene set inside a house is followed by a scene set in a garden. If this happens in a play you are performing, make sure your set can be changed very quickly.

Stratford-upon-Avon

The most famous playwright in the English language is William Shakespeare.

He was born in the English town of Stratford-upon-Avon in 1564. The town is now a major tourist destination, with many of the buildings that were around in Shakespeare's day still standing and open to the public.

15

From the Page to the Stage

In a huge warehouse, which is used as a storeroom for sets, this set designer is working on the set designs for an opera.

And here's the finished set on opening night! Doesn't it look great?

3 Budget

Wishing for a Million!

Several times while we were building our set we wished we had a million dollars. Then we could have built the best set in the world!

Our budget: $200!

Things to do

• sketch the sets
• buy props to make the sets
• find people to help!

Sets Required

• a skyscraper
• a market

But of course we didn't have a million dollars. In fact, we had a budget of just $200. So we had to make a lot of smart, money-wise decisions.

Design Comes Before Building

A set has to be designed before it is built. Professional theater companies often spend more than $200 just building a model of their set! In order to save money, we decided not to buy cardboard, glue, and other materials to build a model. Instead, we saved money by drawing sketches of our set.

We thought our marketplace set would look like these sketches.

Warming Up

Acting is a very physical activity. Actors have to warm up their bodies for the same reasons that sports stars warm up before an event. They have to make sure their body can stand up to the pressure. One area of the body that gets very close attention during an actor's warm-up is the voice.

Recycling Sets

Our director told us that opera companies store their sets in huge warehouses and reuse the materials whenever they can. A large piece of wood may have been painted and used as background scenery for a palace in one opera, and then repainted to show a ship at sea in another opera.

It's cheaper to paint over existing sets than build new ones!

Creating a Skyscraper

Once we had drawn sketches of our set, we had to decide which materials we needed to turn these plans into a real set.

We were really innovative. We decided that we could stack boxes on top of each other and cover them with cloth to create a skyscraper.

We think our skyscraper is great!

Asking Around

When we had made a list of everything we required, we asked friends, parents, and local businesses if they could donate or lend us any of the materials. Everyone was willing to help. Our skyscraper cost us nothing! A local shop sent us their old boxes, while someone's parents had a huge piece of cloth lying around at home.

We built our skyscraper from just these items!

Spending Wisely

We did have to buy some materials and we kept track of the cost of everything. Our stage manager was responsible for the money. If someone needed to buy an item, that person would ask the stage manager for some money. Everyone always had to ask for receipts. This is what the final budget looked like.

Our Budget

2	cans of paint	
4	paintbrushes	$42.50
2	buckets	$32.25
2	tubes of glue	$8.80
4	large wooden poles	$9.90
12	sheets of cardboard	$28.40
1	packet of felt pens	$26.40
1	potted plant	$7.75
8	fence palings	$19.95
Total		$24.00
		$199.95

Wired for Sound

Have you ever wondered how actors know when they are required on stage? Well, a speaker system links the stage manager to the dressing room. When an actor is just about due on stage, the stage manager speaks into a microphone and says, "Mr Shakespeare, this is your 30-second warning."

4 Time

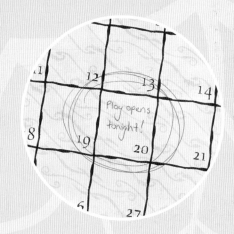

Days or Weeks?

How much time do you have before opening night? Time is very important in determining what your final set will look like. If you have a few weeks, you will be able to build something very elaborate. If you only have a few days, you will have to make sure that your set is easy to construct.

Uh-oh! Only a couple of days until opening night!

Taking Shortcuts

If you don't have much time to build your set, take some shortcuts. Paint trees or buildings on a backdrop, rather than making realistic-looking trees and buildings. If a scene takes place on a street, build a street sign rather than creating the whole street. The audience will still understand where the scene is taking place.

Doesn't our set look different from our original set sketches? (see page 19)

Theater Around the World

Most cultures around the world have their own forms of theater. In Japan, Kabuki is a popular form of theater. Only men perform Kabuki. In Indonesia, Wayang Kulit theater involves the use of shadow puppets. Vietnam is famous for its water puppetry, which has been around for over 1,000 years.

Lighting and Sound

Lighting and sound are great time-savers. If a scene in your play calls for thunder and lightning, get someone to flick the lights on and off while musicians bang drums and clash cymbals. You can also place colored plastic over some of the lights to create particular atmospheres.

Blue light creates a cool atmosphere.

Simple musical instruments will be perfect for sound effects off stage!

Experience

The best way to build a set if you only have a short time is to get as many people involved as you can. This includes parents, other family members, and friends. Everybody has a special talent. Find out what each person can do and then set them to work.

List of special talents and experience

Angela's mum is great at cutting material.

Tom's brother works as a carpenter (he can saw the wood).

Alex's uncle works as a painter (he can paint the wood).

Rachel's friend Deb is very good at sewing.

Types of Arts

There are three main forms of arts: performing, visual, and written. Theater is one of three performing arts. The others are dance and music. The visual arts include painting, photography, and sculpture. The written arts include novels and poetry.

5 Imagination

Communicating Messages

Although sets are an important part of theater, they should not be the only focus of your attention. Theater is about communicating messages. It is also about transporting the audience to a different world. The best way to do this is through imagination.

The Ekkyklema

Technology in theater is nothing new. The ancient Greeks used a device called an ekkyklema, which was a wheeled platform that moved scenery and performers onto a stage. Audiences understood that action that took place on the ekkyklema represented action indoors.

A Long List

Our play required a scene set in a crowded marketplace. We spent a long time discussing what we should put on stage to represent the market. We made a list that included tables, food, mats and rugs, clothing racks, and piles of books. The list went on and on! There were so many things we had to find or buy, that we decided to do the scene another way.

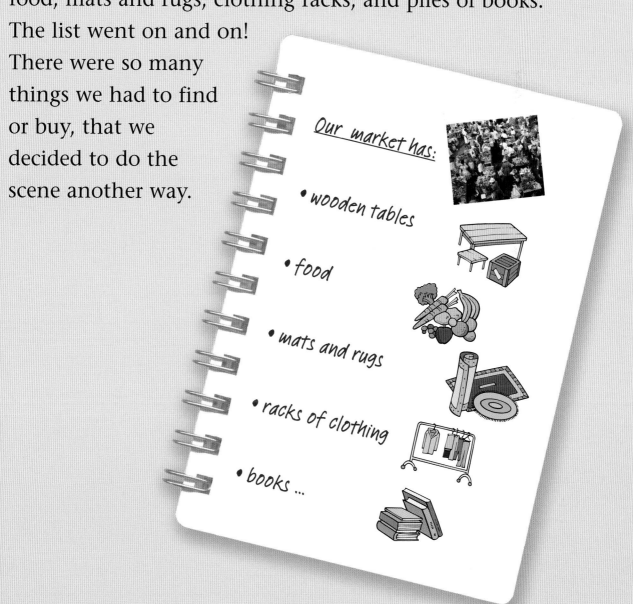

Our market has:

• wooden tables

• food

• mats and rugs

• racks of clothing

• books ...

Pretending

Our director had a great idea for the market scene. It involved hardly any props, no set, and no special lighting. Only the actors and the stage were needed! We recreated a crowded market by behaving as if we were in a market and pretending we were handling goods. It took a lot of rehearsing to make the mimes convincing.

Rachel is waiting for a friend to meet her at the market.

Angela is selling Tom a shirt. Tom is giving her money.

Our market scene didn't need any of these.

A market has:
- wooden tables
- food
- mats and rugs
- racks of clothing
- books ...

The Power of Theater

After we performed our play, most audience members told us they liked the market scene best. Our acting had been so realistic that the audience actually believed they were in the middle of a crowded market. That's the power of theater at work.

Alex is holding up a big bag of apples.

Science as Theater

Science and scientists have been the subject of many plays. One of the most recent is *Copenhagen* by Michael Frayn. When writing his play, Frayn was not sure whether audiences would understand what the main characters were talking about. "When I started writing the play, I didn't think anyone would actually come and see it," he said. He needn't have worried. *Copenhagen* won an award for Best Play for the Year 2000.

Index

Bookweb Links

Read more Bookweb 4 titles about theater, entertainment, and acting:

Understudies—Fiction

A Stage He's Going Through—Fiction

Sally Spylaw and the Flower Shop Mystery—Fiction

Backstage Pass—Nonfiction

Key to Bookweb Fact Boxes

- ■ Arts
- ■ Health
- ■ Science
- ■ Social Studies
- ■ Technology